THE SUPREME COURT OF HEAVEN

GLEN FERGUSON

Copyright © 2021 by Glen Ferguson
All rights reserved.

Contents

Introduction.. 1
Chapter 1.. 5
Chapter 2... 11
Chapter 3... 17
Chapter 4... 23
Chapter 5... 29
Chapter 6... 37
Chapter 7... 43
Chapter 8... 51
Chapter 9... 57
Chapter 10.. 63
Chapter 11.. 69
Chapter 12.. 77
Chapter 13.. 83
Chapter 14.. 89

Introduction

As we look into this amazing subject, may the Lord and judge of all, give us insight and revelation about "The Supreme Court of Heaven"!

Some may be baffled, others unsure and sceptical and there will be those who simply do not believe, but I will suggest that you have an open mind as you read and study this word.

In the same way that the nations of this world have boundaries and laws, which govern their citizens, for those who break the set boundaries, rules and laws, they must face the consequences!

Law-breakers are brought before the courts and judicial systems of the country, where judgements are passed and imposed, equally there is a judicial system in heaven, of which the earthly system is a type!

In preparation for the building of the tabernacle Moses is told in Exodus 25:40 *"And look that thou make them after their pattern, which was shewed thee in the mount"!*

On Mount Sinai Moses actually "Saw" the tabernacle, the dwelling place of God, which he was instructed to ensure that he built to the exact specification of what was shown to him!

He "Saw" something of the heavenly which God wanted to replicate on the earth.

"According to all that I shew thee, after the pattern of the tabernacle and the pattern of all the instruments thereof, even so shall ye make it"! (Exodus 25:9)

Note the wording of Hebrew 8:1-2

"Now of the things which we have spoken, this is the sum, we have such an high priest, who is set on the right hand of the throne of the majesty in the heavens"! (V1)

"A minister of the sanctuary and of the true tabernacle, which the Lord pitched and not man"! (V2)

"This is the sum…" says the writer of Hebrews, this is the point, this is the main thing, this is what it is all about!

In the Old Testament there was a high priest, an earthly intermediary or advocate, one who stood in the gap and spoke to God on the behalf of the people!

But; in heaven you and I also have a high priest, "Who is set on the right hand of the throne of the majesty in the heavens"!

This high priest is our intercessor and advocate in the true tabernacle, the likes of which the earthly tabernacle and priesthood is only a type and our advocate is none other than the Lord Jesus Christ!

As you go through the pages of this book my prayer is that like Hilkiah the high priest, you will declare *"I have found the book of the Law in the house of the Lord".* (2 Kings 22:8)

ACKNOWLEDGEMENTS

Unless otherwise stated, all Biblical references used in this book is taken from the King James version.

I would also like to thank the following people for their help in the compiling and completion of this book:

Chris Kembrey, for her kindness and long hours spent in the proofreading of this work and the description of the book on the back page.

Darren Ferguson and Justin Atherley for the front cover design.

PJ Ashiru for her patience and diligence in the formatting of this book.

DEDICATION

I would like to dedicate this book to my Faith Dimensions Church, who has stood by my wife and I through turbulent and difficult times.

May the Lord Jesus Christ who is your intercessor and advocate in "The Supreme Court of Heaven" protect and defend you from the accuser, who seeks to discredit and disqualify you from receiving the blessings of God in your life!

Chapter 1

Zechariah 3:1- 4

"And He shewed me Joshua the high priest standing before the angel of the Lord and Satan standing at his right hand to resist him"! (V1)

"And the Lord said unto Satan, the Lord rebuke thee, O Satan, even the Lord that hath chosen Jerusalem rebuke thee, is not this a branch plucked out of the fire?"! (V2)

"Now Joshua was clothed with filthy garments and stood before the angel"! (V3)

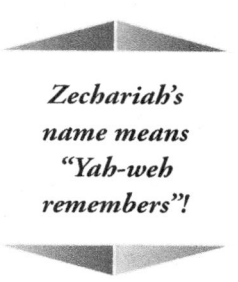

Zechariah's name means "Yah-weh remembers"!

"And He answered and spake unto those that stood before Him saying, take away the filthy garments from him and unto him He said, behold I have caused thine iniquity to pass from thee and I will clothe thee with change of raiment"! (V4)

There were three prophets who spoke on the behalf of God to His people at that time, they were Haggai, Malachi and Zechariah!

He was called by God and assigned the task of reminding the Jews that He God, remembered them as they returned from their many years of captivity and exile!

THE SUPREME COURT OF HEAVEN

Among the prophecies given by Zechariah the most exciting of all was the promise of the coming of the Messiah, who would set up His eternal kingdom!

Zechariah is given a glimpse into the supernatural realm where he sees a heavenly courtroom, where Joshua, stood accused and resisted by the prosecutor, Satan!

What was he being accused of? Breaking the law, which God Himself had instituted in Exodus 28:2 *"And thou shalt make holy garments for Aaron thy brother, for glory and for beauty"!*

Believers, this is all about the heart being clean and pure!

Note verse 29 of the same chapter *"And Aaron shall bear the names of the children of Israel in the breastplate of judgement upon his heart, when he goeth in unto the holy place, for a memorial before the Lord continually"!*

Believers; it is important to know that there can and will be no glory or beauty without righteousness and sinless living, this is all about the heart being clean and pure! *"And Aaron shall bear the names of the children of Israel in the breastplate of judgement upon his heart..."!*

When Joshua therefore appeared before the Lord in His Supreme Court wearing "filthy garments" Satan resisted him based on the Law of God.

There was no exemption clause in the Law which allowed or permitted the high priest to stand before the Judge wearing or being clothed in filthy garments. Therefore, the accuser had legitimate reasons and grounds for his accusation against both Joshua and Judah.

Joshua stood or operated in the role of intercessor on behalf of his people Judah, but when he tried to outline his case, Satan, the prosecuting lawyer and accuser, stood at his right hand and declared, "You have no defence."

> *Greed, jealousy and materialism can bring poverty and lack into one's life.*

Most intercessors approach the whole business of intercession and prayer with great fervency as they stand in the gap for others and declare: "Satan, I bind you in the name of Jesus."

This is a very big problem. Why you may ask? Let me give you a few examples:

- Legally, unforgiveness can bring sickness in one's life.
- Pride can cause a person to be brought very low.
- Greed, jealousy and materialism can bring poverty and lack into one's life.

When the intercessor attacks Satan, who opposes and resists a person based on legitimate grounds, not only will the person they are praying for not experience release and deliverance, but the demons of hell will also come against the intercessor.

More often than not, before there can be any binding of demonic strongholds in a person's life, that person has to first be brought to a place of forgiveness and repentance; unforgiveness is a huge stumbling block in the way of deliverance.

Jesus our Defence Lawyer *"And the Lord said unto Satan, The Lord rebuke thee, O Satan." (Zech 3:2)* I am not only the Law-giver, I am also the Law-maker, I am Jehovah, the self-existing one.

> **Unforgiveness is a huge stumbling block in the way of deliverance**

Yes, it is true that Joshua is dressed in filthy garments, but what you don't seem to understand is this: he is a branch that has been plucked out of the fire, and so also are those he represents. Judah has been plucked or delivered from the fire of their Babylonian captivity, and this is a dress rehearsal for another 'branch' which is to come.

"Hear now, O Joshua the high priest, thou and thy fellows that sit before thee, for they are men wondered at: for behold I will bring forth my servant the branch." (Zech 3:8)

Isaiah also prophesied about that branch in Isaiah 11:1, *"And there shall come forth a rod out of the stem of Jesse, and a branch shall grow out of his roots."*

Here comes the Branch, out of the root of Jesse; Jesse begat David, out of David came Solomon and Roboam. The root kept on growing until Matthew tells us in chapter 1:17, *"...and from David until the carrying away into Babylon are fourteen generations; and from the carrying away into Babylon unto Christ are fourteen generations."*

When the Branch finally broke through, the one of whom the prophets prophesied, appeared, and John the Baptist declared: *"...Behold the Lamb of God which taketh away the sin of the world." (John 1:29)*

The Judge says, "...*Take away the filthy garment from him (Joshua). And unto him he said, Behold, I have caused thine iniquity to pass from thee, and I will clothe thee with change of raiment.*" *(Zech 3:4)*

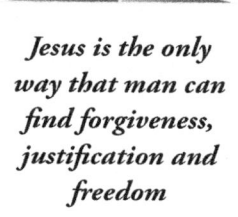

Jesus is the only way that man can find forgiveness, justification and freedom

The removal by Joshua of his filthy garments would not appease the Judge. The only way that Joshua, who represented Judah could be acquitted would be if someone else, namely man's advocate and intercessor in 'The Supreme Court of Heaven', the Lord Jesus Himself, would show mercy on the accused. This is the only way that man can find forgiveness, justification and freedom!

"*And the Lord said unto Satan, The Lord rebuke thee, O Satan…*" *(Zech 3:2)*

The Judge and Law-giver, hearing the appeal of our Advocate, has declared, "*…Behold, I have caused thine… iniquity to pass from thee and I will clothe thee with change of raiment.*" *(Zech 3:4)*

Therefore, we are forgiven and acquitted, our case is dismissed!

Chapter 2

Acts 12:1-5

"Now about that time Herod the king stretched forth his hands to vex certain of the church." (v1)

"And he killed James the brother of John with the sword." (v2)

"And because he saw it pleased the Jews, he proceeded further to take Peter also. (Then were the days of unleavened bread)." (v3)

"And when he had apprehended him, he put him in prison and delivered him to four quaternions of soldiers to keep him; intending after Easter to bring him forth to the people." (v4)

Peter therefore was kept in prison: but prayer was made without ceasing of the Church unto God for him. (Acts12 v 5)

"Peter therefore was kept in prison: but prayer was made without ceasing of the Church unto God for him." (v5)

Eight years of relative peace for the Church came to an abrupt end. The devil entered into Herod, the grandson of Herod the Great, the one who tried to kill Jesus in His infancy.

Herod Agrippa 1 was also the nephew of Herod Antipas, the one who murdered John the Baptist.

So, the devil decided to come against God's people; he induced Herod to behead James, the brother of John.

James was the second apostle to be martyred for following Jesus the Messiah; and was killed with the sword. Stephen was the first martyr; he was stoned to death.

Please note the words at the end of verse 3, *"Then were the days of unleavened bread."*

The intention of Herod to kill Peter was interrupted and put on-hold because of the event which was happening at the same time as Peter's arrest.

> *The days of unleavened bread, is a reference to the Passover which commemorates the release of the Jews from Egypt.*

The days of unleavened bread, is a reference to the Passover, the Greek word for Passover is "Pes-ach". It commemorates the release and exodus of the Jews from Egypt, the land of bondage, oppression and slavery.

Exodus 12:22-23

"And ye shall take a bunch of hyssop and dip it in the blood that is in the bason and strike the lintel and the two side posts with the blood that is in the bason and none of you shall go out of the door of his house until the morning." (v22)

"For the LORD will pass through to smite the Egyptians and when he seeth the blood upon the lintel and on the two side posts, the LORD will pass over the door and will not suffer the destroyer to come in unto your houses to smite you." (v23)

Peter was on death row but it was the time of the Passover; the time of commemoration and celebration of what God had done for His people in releasing them from captivity.

Thousands of pilgrims had headed towards Jerusalem in preparation for the great celebration, this is why Herod's plans had to be put on hold.

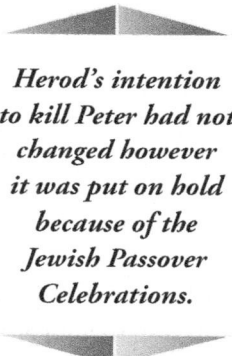

Herod's intention to kill Peter had not changed however it was put on hold because of the Jewish Passover Celebrations.

According to history, Herod Agrippa 1 was a king of Judah, he was not a member of the Sanhedrin, who were the judicial body of the day. What was he therefore doing killing James, and now arresting Peter and having the same intention towards him?

Let me reiterate: Herod's intention towards Peter had not changed, it had simply been paused. Peter's life and future on the earth was now in the balance, unless something drastic happened in the next three days he too would lose his life.

"The Supreme Court of Heaven"

"Peter therefore was kept in prison, but prayer was made without ceasing of the Church unto God for him." (Acts 12:5)

A judgement and sentence had already been passed, which resulted in the execution and death of James and now the same judge Herod, had the same intention and plan for Peter.

Here, in verse 5, we see the Church approaching another court on behalf of their beloved Peter, *"...but prayer was made without ceasing of the Church unto God for him."*

There is no doubting the fact that Herod the king was lining up the court of Palestine to agree with him and pronounce a judgement of guilty and pass a sentence of death to Peter.

> *In the Supreme Court of Heaven, whatever the Judge of all spirits passes is final!*

But unbeknown to the Church, when they took his case to God in prayer, they entered into another court room, one which was no less real than the courtrooms of this world, they entered into "The Supreme Court of Heaven".

This is the ultimate of courts, this is the place where whatever the Judge of all spirits passes, is final!

As the Church looked to the heavens for answers and a change to what they knew was awaiting Peter, as they pleaded his case, the Judge having heard their defence argument, judged Peter guiltless and vindicated him.

He therefore despatched one of His guardian angels to the earth.

"And, behold, the angel of the Lord came upon him, and a light shined in the prison: and he smote Peter on the side, and raised him up, saying, Arise up quickly. And his chains fell off from his hands." (Acts 12:7)

This is absolutely extraordinary, the Church did not appeal to Herod and the Palestinian court, they appealed to God, the Judge of "The Supreme Court of Heaven".

In desperation the Church made importunity to God, who overturned Herod's plans for Peter, the result of which was the assigning of a mighty celestial being who could not be stopped or restricted by earthly chains or bars.

The angel did not need the aid of earthly lights to see, "…a light shined in the prison…" neither did he need the earthly keys for the chains which bound Peter to release him, "…up quickly and his chains fell off from his hands."

The Church appealed to God on behalf of Peter and the Lord assigned a mighty celestial being who could not be stopped or restricted by earthly chains or bars.

Chapter 3

Acts 25:6-12

"And when he had tarried among them more than ten days, he went down unto Caesarea; and the next day sitting on the judgement seat commanded Paul to be brought." (v6)

"And when he was come, the Jews which came down from Jerusalem stood round bout and laid many and grievous complaints against Paul, which they could not prove." (v7)

"While he answered for himself, neither against the law of the Jews, neither against the temple, nor yet against Caesar have I offended any thing at all." (v8)

"But Festus, willing to do the Jews a pleasure, answered Paul and said, Wilt thou go up to Jerusalem, and there be judged of these things before me?" (v9)

"Then said Paul, I stand at Caesar's judgement seat, where I ought to be judged: to the Jews have I done no wrong, as thou very well knowest." (v10)

"For if I be an offender or have committed anything worthy of death, I refuse not to die, but if there be none of those things whereof these accuse me, no man may deliver me unto them. I appeal to Caesar." (v11)

THE SUPREME COURT OF HEAVEN

"Then Festus, when he had conferred with the council, answered, Hast thou appealed unto Caesar? Unto Caesar shalt thou go." (v12)

The hierarchy of the law courts in the UK are:

- Magistrates court
- Crown court
- Courts of appeal
- Supreme or high court.

In the lower court's judges are referred to as, "Your honour", whereas in the high courts they are referred to as, "My lord" or "Your lordship".

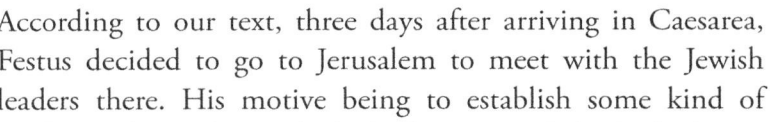

The decisions made in the Supreme courts are final and cannot be overruled by any other judicial authority within this country or nation.

The decisions made in the Supreme courts are final and cannot be overruled by any other judicial authority within this country or nation.

According to our text, three days after arriving in Caesarea, Festus decided to go to Jerusalem to meet with the Jewish leaders there. His motive being to establish some kind of working relationship with the high priest and the Sanhedrin.

The Jewish leaders wanted Festus to send Paul back to Jerusalem for a trial. Verse 2 of Acts 25 says, *"Then the high priest and the chief of the Jews informed him against Paul, and besought him."* They literally begged and petitioned him.

This they did not because they were interested in any kind of legal proceeding or trial, their motive was far more sinister. Acts 23:12-14, tells us what their motive was: *"And when it was day, certain of the Jews banded together and bound themselves under a curse saying that they would neither eat or drink till they had killed Paul." (v12)*

"And they were more than forty which had made this conspiracy." (v13)

"And they came to the chief priest's and elders and said, we have bound ourselves under a great curse that we will eat nothing until we have slain Paul." (v14)

The fact that these forty men included fasting in their resolve to kill Paul meant that they were also drawing on the supernatural power of demons to aid them in their desire and attempt; they feared Paul and whatever power that was with him.

> *These forty men included fasting in their resolve to kill Paul which meant that they were also drawing on the supernatural power of demons to aid them in their desire and attempt.*

Previously Felix was the Roman procurator or governor of Judea, he was the one who arrested Paul in the first place! *"I will hear thee, said he, when thine accusers are also come. And he commanded him to be kept in Herod's judgement hall." (Acts 23:35)*

Felix is now superseded by Festus, and it is Festus who reopens Paul's case, and in an attempt to please the Jewish leaders, he asked Paul, *"... Wilt thou go up to Jerusalem and be there judged of these things before me?" (Acts 25:9)*

Paul responded, *"I stand at Caesar's judgement seat where I ought to be judged, to the Jews have I done no wrong, as thou very well knowest." (v10)*

It was the right of all citizens of Rome who were accused of breaking the law to have their case heard and tried in their own homeland of Rome.

When Paul further declared in *Acts 25:11*, *"...I appeal unto Caesar"*, it meant that his case could only be heard in the higher courts of Caesarea and not in Jerusalem.

> *When Paul appealed unto Caesar, it meant that his case could only be heard in the higher courts of Caesarea and not in Jerusalem.*

Festus was out of his depth, when Paul made his declaration. It cornered him legally. He therefore had to bring Paul's case to the higher authority of King Agrippa.

Acts 25:13-15

"And after certain days king Agrippa and Bernice came unto Caesarea to salute Festus." (v13)

"And when they had been there many days, Festus declared Paul's cause unto the king saying, There is a certain man left in bonds by Felix" (v14)

"About whom, when I was at Jerusalem, the chief priests and the elders of the Jews informed me, desiring to have judgement against him." (v15)

If Paul had agreed to have his case tried by Festus in Jerusalem, he would not have had a fair trial, because of the Jews hatred and false allegation of treason, which they had drummed up against him. They wanted him dead.

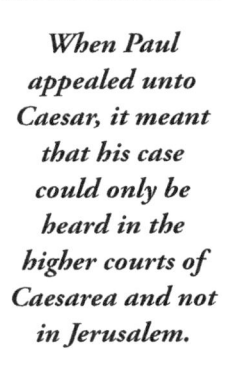

Agrippa permits Paul to speak in Acts 26:1-3,6

"Then Agrippa said unto Paul, thou art permitted to speak for thyself, then Paul stretched forth his hand and answered for himself." (v1)

"I think myself happy, king Agrippa, because I shall answer for myself this day before thee touching all the things whereof, I am accused of the Jews." (v2)

> **Paul would not have had a fair trial in Jerusalem because of the Jews hatred and their false allegation of treason against him.**

"Especially because I know thee to be an expert in all customs and questions which are among the Jews, wherefore I beseech thee to hear me patiently." (v3)

Note also *verse 6, "And now I stand and am judged for the hope of the promise made of God unto our fathers."*

I want to highlight three things from the four verses above:

- When accused by our enemies and the demons of hell, we must speak up in faith.
- Our God and King is an expert in all matters of the Law, in fact He is the Law-maker.
- You and I are accused because of the hope and promise given first to our fathers. Due to the fact that we believe, and hold firmly to the same, the enemy of our soul accuses us.

They have and will continue to fail in their attempt to cause the Judge to pronounce, "Guilty as charged."

Their accusations will not succeed because Jesus, our Lord, has already declared in the "Supreme Court of Heaven", "Case dismissed!"

When accused by our enemies and the demons of hell, we must speak up in faith.

Chapter 4

Acts 26:1-3

"Then Agrippa said unto Paul, thou art permitted to speak for thyself. Then Paul stretched forth the hand and answered for himself" (v1)

"I think myself happy, king Agrippa, because I shall answer for myself this day before thee touching all the things whereof I am accused of the Jews" (v2)

"Especially because I know thee to be expert in all customs and questions which are among the Jews, wherefore I beseech thee to hear me patiently." (v3)

King Agrippa charged Paul to speak and declare his case before the court, he wanted to hear Paul's side of the argument.

What Agrippa was actually saying here in verse 1 is, 'Paul, I can do nothing for you unless or until you speak for yourself. Let me hear your side of the argument or story. I have heard the words of those who have accused you, now it's your turn, you must speak and declare your case.'

In that day it was customary for a prisoner to raise his hand, to the court and judge, as an act of appreciation and acknowledgement of the privilege and honour to be able to speak and defend themselves.

THE SUPREME COURT OF HEAVEN

Being pleased to have been given the opportunity to bear witness of the things of which he was accused, Paul therefore came straight to the point.

His purpose was twofold:

- To defend himself.
- To be a witness for the Lord Jesus Christ.

Being king of the Jews, Herod Agrippa was very familiar and versed in the Jewish laws and customs.

Paul knew that in matters concerning the law, Agrippa was far more qualified than Festus.

He knew that his only chance of receiving a fair hearing was to have his case heard in Caesarea and not in Jerusalem, as requested by the priests and the Jews.

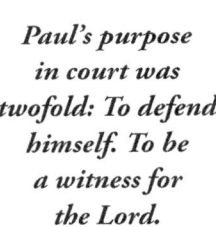

Paul's purpose in court was twofold: To defend himself. To be a witness for the Lord.

He knew that his case had to be heard in another place and before the one who was an expert in all matters of the law and customs.

Paul's life was very orthodox:

- He was born in Tarsus.
- Educated in Jerusalem and taught by Gamaliel the greatest Jewish teacher of the day.
- He was a Pharisee, the strictest of religious sects.

One of the most cherished and hoped for beliefs among the Jews was the promise that God would one day send the Messiah.

Ironically, the main charge brought against Paul by the priests and the Jews, was the very promise in which both they and Paul believed.

The only difference between what they believed and what Paul believed was:

- They were looking for and believed that the Messiah was yet to come, they were longing for His arrival.
- Paul, on the other hand, believed that the Messiah had already come, he said in verse 6, *"And now I stand and am judged for the hope of the promise made of God unto our fathers."*

> *One of the most cherished and hoped for beliefs among the Jews was the promise that God would one day send the Messiah.*

Between Acts 26:6-23 Paul expounded and explained his experience of meeting the risen Christ, the promised Messiah.

This was what Festus was referring to when he spoke to Agrippa about Paul's accusers in Acts 25:19, *"But had certain questions against him of their own superstition and one Jesus, which was dead, whom Paul affirmed to be alive."*

While others were still looking for Him, Paul was absolutely adamant and sure, that due to the fact that he had personally met the crucified Jesus on the Damascus road, and the fact that He had risen from the dead, proved Jesus was the awaited, promised Messiah and Lord.

Paul told Agrippa about the blinding light from heaven and the audible voice which spoke to him at the time of his encounter.

He spoke about the Jews who caught him in the temple and tried to kill him.

I love what he says in Acts 26:22, *"Having therefore obtained help from God, I continue unto this day, witnessing both to small and great, saying none other things than those which the prophets and Moses did say should come."*

> **Paul told Agrippa about the blinding light from heaven and the audible voice which spoke to him at the time of his encounter.**

What Moses and the prophets had said, Paul had now experienced, and it was that experience which motivated him to do the things which he was now doing.

One of the saddest verses in the Bible comes at the end of Paul's defence before Agrippa. It is when Agrippa, who although convicted by what he had heard from Paul, responded in verse 28, *"Then Agrippa said unto Paul, almost thou persuades me to be a Christian."*

How very sad, "almost", so close, yet so far from being a child of the living God and entering into His kingdom.

Being convicted by the Holy Spirit and not yielding or surrendering one's life to Him, is not only sad, it is tragic. It leaves the individual in a state of unending condemnation and facing an eternity separated from the one who came to give joy, peace and hope.

As you speak and raise your case in "the Supreme Court of Heaven" know that the One you are speaking to is an expert in all matters of the Law.

Be confident that in spite of the fact that the devil and his demons are always accusing you, when the trial is over, like Paul, you will testify, "I have obtained help of God."

Being convicted by the Holy Spirit and not yielding or surrendering one's life to Him, is not only sad, it is tragic.

Chapter 5

Ezekiel 22:30-31

"And I sought for a man among them that should make up the hedge and stand in the gap before me for the land, that I should not destroy it, but I found none." (v30)

"Therefore have I poured out mine indignation upon them, I have consumed them with the fire of my wrath, their own way have I recompensed upon their heads, saith the Lord God" (v31)

In verse 28 the Lord said the prophets, *"...have daubed them with untempered morter."*

> **Those prophets were involved in false prophesies, promising blessings and declaring what the Lord had not said.**

Untempered mortar is mud-plaster or whitewash, it is an inferior material. Those prophets were involved in false prophesies, promising blessings and declaring: "Thus sayeth the Lord God," when the Lord had not spoken.

They used the word of God as a means of profiteering and looting, but the Lord, the Judge had already said in Ezekiel 13:14, *"So I will break down the wall that ye have daubed with untempered morter and bring it down..."*

The very same thing happened in the days when Jesus walked the earth. Listen to His condemning words against such people:

"Woe unto you scribes and Pharisees, hypocrites! for ye are like unto whited sepulchres, which indeed appear beautiful outward, but are within full of dead men's bones and of all uncleanness." (Matt 23:27)

The ministry of intercession is crucially important in the Church today, it is the Supreme Judge's prescribed method of averting judgement, disaster and death.

> *The ministry of intercession is God's prescribed method of averting judgement, disaster and death.*

In spite of the magnitude and the gravity of the assignment and calling, the Judge and Law-maker, God Himself has set the ministry of the intercessor in His Church as a means of silencing the voice of the accuser.

Ezekiel 33:1-6

"Again the word of the Lord came unto me, saying," (v1)

"Son of man, speak to the children of thy people, and say unto them, When I bring the sword upon a land, if the people of the land take a man of their coasts, and set him for their watchman" (v2)

"if when he seeth the sword come upon the land, he blow the trumpet, and warn the people" (v3)

"Then whosoever heareth the sound of the trumpet, and taketh not warning, if the sword come and take him away, his blood shall be upon his own head." (v4)

"He heard the sound of the trumpet, and took not warning, his blood shall be upon him, but he that taketh warning shall deliver his soul." (v5)

"But if the watchman see the sword come, and blow not the trumpet, and the people be not warned; if the sword come and take any person from among them, he is taken away in his iniquity, but his blood will I require at the watchman's hand." (v6)

Believers, Babylon is not our destiny, God has a better place and plan for us.

"...the children of thy people..." (v2) is in reference to those Jews, who like Ezekiel himself, were captured by Nebuchadnezzar and were exiled in Babylon.

In other words, Ezekiel was well placed to understand the plight of the people. Believers, Babylon is not our destiny, God has a better place and plan for us.

Our Lord and King did not deliver us out of Egypt for us, once again, to be captured and ensnared in or by Babylon.

He took us out of the darkness of this world that He might bring us into His marvellous and glorious light and kingdom.

I stand in the place and office of the intercessor because I see the sword of God coming in the land and as such, I now blow the trumpet and declare, he that hath an ear let him hear. These are dark and dangerous days, you must therefore save yourselves from that which is to come.

There will be one of two reactions to the blowing of the trumpet and the voice of the intercessor:

"Then whosoever heareth the sound of the trumpet and taketh not warning, if the sword come and take him away, his blood shall be upon his own head." (v4)

> *These are dark and dangerous days, you must therefore save yourselves from that which is to come.*

"...But he that taketh warning shall deliver his soul." (v5)

We are talking about "The Supreme Court of Heaven" and if we go right back to the beginning of the Bible, we see a law being instituted by God the Creator and Judge. *"But of the tree of the knowledge of good and evil, thou shalt not eat of it, for in the day that thou eatest thereof, thou shalt surely die." (Gen 2:17)*

We know that Adam and Eve died spiritually. This man and his wife, who the Creator would come down in the cool of the day and have fellowship with, broke the instituted law and could no longer relate to Him.

Note these tragic words in Genesis 3:8, *"...and Adam and his wife hid themselves from the presence of the Lord God amongst the trees of the garden."*

> *Adam and Eve broke God's instituted law. As a result, they died spiritually and could no longer relate to their Creator.*

Verse 7 of the same chapter tells us, *"And the eyes of them both were opened, and they knew that they were naked..."*

They were always naked, but they were unaware of it because they were covered by the glory and grace of God their Creator.

Oh, the tragedy of sin, it removes innocence and reveals shame, it makes one aware of the ugliness of a life without the protection of God.

It took the shedding of blood to restore Adam and Eve, Genesis 3:21, *"Unto Adam also and unto his wife did the Lord God make coats of skin, and clothed them."*

Adam and Eve doubted and questioned the word of God, the result of which was the entire human race being plunged into a world and life of sin and separation from God.

Ezekiel 22:30 says, "And I sought for a man among them that should make up the hedge and stand in the gap before me for the land, that I should not destroy it, but I found none."

This is all a question of law that we are talking about here, in the days of Ezekiel God sought for a man to stand in the gap. He looked for an intercessor, one who would be an Intermediary between judgement and freedom, but He found none.

> **The Lord looked for an Intercessor, one who would be an Intermediary between judgement and freedom, but He found none.**

Due to the fact that Eve, the mother of all living, was a woman, if God was going to bring hope, redemption and salvation to a lost and dying humanity through a man, He would first have to find a woman who would birth such a man.

- Sarah could not be that woman; she was too cynical and unbelieving.
- Deborah could not be that woman; she was too violent.

- Naomi could not be that woman; she was too despondent and discouraged.

It is not until we get over into the book of Luke that we see God finally finding a woman, actually a young girl who was a virgin, that He could use to fulfil His plan of salvation for mankind.

Luke 1:26-27

"And in the sixth month the angel Gabriel was sent from God, unto a city of Galilee, named Nazareth" (v26)

"To a virgin espoused to a man whose name was Joseph, of the house of David; and the virgin's name was Mary." (v27)

Gabriel, one of heaven's messengers, was sent from "The Supreme Court of Heaven" as an ambassador to the earth, to a specific city and town and to a specific and chosen woman.

Gabriel, one of heaven's messengers, was sent from "The Supreme Court of Heaven" as an ambassador to the earth to a specific and chosen woman called Mary.

He was sent to someone, who was untouched by man, with an incredible message and assignment from the Judge and Law-maker of heaven.

The assignment was: "Will you be willing to be the conduit and channel through which the Redeemer and Messiah could come?"

Mary's response Luke 1:38, *"...Behold the handmaid of the Lord, be it unto me according to thy word..."*

I am sure Mary had some questions about all that was being said to her, but what God wanted was her compliance and obedience because, "For with God nothing shall be impossible" (v37).

- In the days of Babylonian captivity, God found a man, an intercessor in the person of Ezekiel to send His prophetic word.
- In the days of the Messiah, God found a vessel in the person of Mary, through whom Jesus came.

As you read this book, "The Supreme Court of Heaven", may the Lord and God of heaven find in you a willingness to say, as Mary, "Be it unto me according to thy word."

Chapter 6

Exodus 25:8-10, and 26:30

25:8, "And let them make me a sanctuary; that I may dwell among them."

25:9, "According to all that I shew thee, after the pattern of the tabernacle, and the pattern of all the instruments thereof, even so shall ye make it"

25:10, "And they shall make an ark of shittim wood: two cubits and a half shall be the length thereof, and a cubit and a half the breath thereof, and a cubit and a half the height thereof."

26:30, "And thou shalt rear up the tabernacle according to the fashion thereof which was shewed thee in the mount."

In Exodus 19:11 we read these incredible words, *"And be ready against the third day, for the third day the LORD will come down in the sight of all the people upon mount Sinai."*

Again, note these words in Exodus 31:18, *"And He gave unto Moses, when he had made an end of communing with him upon mount Sinai, two tables of testimony, tables of stone, written with the finger of God."*

In verse 8 of Exodus 25 the word "sanctuary" is used.

It speaks of a holy, unique and separated place, a place where Jehovah God, whose dwelling is not of this world will come and dwell.

God, whose dwelling is not of this world, His home and dwelling is beyond the visible, natural and material.

This God decided that He wanted to replicate His dwelling place here on the earth, He therefore said to Moses His servant, in verse 9 make it:

"According to all that I shew thee, after the pattern of the tabernacle and the pattern of all the instruments thereof, even so shall ye make it."

"According to all that I shew thee, after the pattern of the tabernacle…"

In dealing with a subject like "The Supreme Court of Heaven" unless the Lord and King, who is the Judge and Master of all, show us, we will never see or understand, and unless we see and understand we cannot enter.

God wanted to replicate His dwelling place here on earth, He therefore instructed Moses to build a Tabernacle according to the specifications He showed him.

The most important piece of furniture in the tabernacle was the Ark of the Covenant; which represented the abiding presence and glory of God among His people.

You may be offering your sacrificial gift on the brazen altar, but unfortunately, in this place, although you may be listen to these words in Hebrews 10:3, "But in those sacrifices there is a remembrance again made of sins, every year."

Until and unless you press through the Holy Place and enter into the Holy of Holies, your life will always be filled with guilt and condemnation, because the accuser always accuses the believer in the courts of heaven.

The only place that the presence of Almighty God dwells, is in the Holy of Holies.

This is the place where the guilty find grace; it is God's appointed place of forgiveness and mercy.

This is the place where the Blood of the Lamb is poured on the mercy seat and in this place the voice of the accuser is silenced.

In Exodus 25:10 God says, *"And they shall make me an ark of shittim wood."* Shittim wood is almost indestructible, it is the most durable and lasting of all wood.

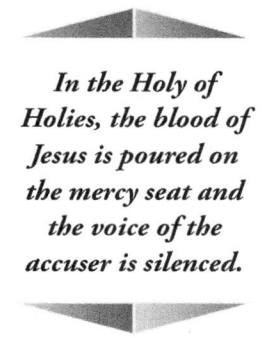

In the Holy of Holies, the blood of Jesus is poured on the mercy seat and the voice of the accuser is silenced.

The word "ark" used here comes from the original Hebrew word "Aw-rone" and was used for the preservation of dead things, for example:

- Joseph was put in the Aw-rone when he died.
- *"So Joseph died, being an hundred and ten years old and they embalmed him and he was put in a coffin in Egypt."* (Gen 50:26)
- The Law, the Ten Commandments was also put in the Aw-rone. *"And thou shalt put into the ark the testimony which I shall give thee."* (Gen 25:16)

There is another word that was used for ark, that is "Taw-baw" in which living things were preserved:

Noah - "And the LORD said unto Noah, Come thou and all thy house into the ark; for thee have I seen righteous before me in this generation." (Gen 7:1)

And Moses - "And when she could not longer hide him, she took for him an ark of bulrushes, and daubed it with slime and with pitch, and put the child therein, and she laid it in the flags by the river's brink." (Ex 2:3)

> **If our sins are buried in the Taw-baw (the ark used for the preservation of living things) we would have no hope of forgiveness and acceptance.**

Believers, I have something exciting to tell you. Since we are dealing with God's judicial system, and specifically, "The Supreme Court of Heaven", if the Judge had buried our sins in the Taw-baw - that which is used for the preservation of living things, we would be in serious trouble; we would have no hope of acceptance and forgiveness, because the accuser would constantly be declaring to the Judge, "Alive, alive, their sins are alive!"

But praise be to God, due to the Blood of the Lamb, our sins are buried in the Aw-rone- that which is used for the preservation of dead things.

Jesus our Lord and Saviour, is both the Lamb of God and our Advocate in "The Supreme Court of Heaven". The accuser brings his case and evidence, before the Judge. You and I are guilty as charged, but praise be to God, because of the finished works of Calvary we are acquitted and set free!

We therefore should not stop speaking about the love and goodness of our gracious God.

"Then they that feared the LORD spake often one to another and the Lord hearkened and heard it, and a book of remembrance was written before him.." (Mal 3:16)

In "The Supreme Court of Heaven" the recording clerk logs the conversations of those who love to talk about the kindness and mercy of the Judge, who has acquitted them of the accusations of the accuser.

By the blood of Jesus, our sins are buried in the Aw-rone *(that which is used for the preservation of dead things.*

Hebrews 9:13-14

"For if the blood of bulls and of goats, and the ashes of an heifer sprinkling the unclean, sanctifieth to the purifying of the flesh" (v13)

"How much more shall the blood of Christ, who through the eternal Spirt offered Himself without spot to God, purge your conscience from dead works, to serve the living God." (v14)

How much more, indeed! The tabernacle made by Moses and Solomon were both temporary, but that which is built by God Himself, is permanent.

If we enter into that room and place, our Defence Lawyer, the Lord Jesus Christ will fight our case and because of His finished work there is no possibility of us losing! Praise be to His glorious name!

Chapter 7

Joshua 7:20-21

"And Achan answered Joshua and said, Indeed I have sinned against the LORD God of Israel and thus and thus have I done." (v20)

"When I saw among the spoils a goodly Babylonish garment and two hundred shekels of silver, and a wedge of gold of fifty shekels weight, then I coveted them and took them and behold they are hid in the earth in the midst of my tent, and the silver under it." (v21)

The word trespass means to commit a violation or to breach the law.

Verse 1 of Joshua 7 begins by telling us that, "…Israel committed a trespass in the accursed thing…"

The word trespass means; to commit a violation, to make a breach of the law.

God had previously warned His people about acquiring any accursed thing.

Joshua 6:18, "And ye in any wise keep yourselves from the accused thing, lest ye make yourselves accursed, when ye take of the accursed thing and make the camp of Israel a curse and trouble it."

The term, accursed or curse is repeated five times between verses 17-18 of Joshua 6. Yet in the midst of the curse, in the midst of the doom and damnation, Rahab the ex-prostitute amazingly found grace, favour and forgiveness.

Joshua 2:18 and 6:25 2:18, "Behold when we come into the land, thou shalt bind this line of scarlet thread in the window which thou didst let us down by and thou shalt bring thy father and thy mother and thy brethren, and all thy father's household, home unto thee."

Rahab, an ex-prostitute received grace, favour and forgiveness from God.

6:25, "And Joshua saved Rahab the harlot alive, and her father's household and all that she had and she dwellleth in Israel, even unto this day, because she hid the messengers which Joshua sent to spy out Jericho."

Unwisely, Achan allowed his lust and craving for the things of the world to cause him to trespass and violate the commandment of God.

He took and hid in his house that which was forbidden. Although out of view, and maybe out of reach, the consequences were nonetheless devastating.

Unbeknown to him, his action gave Satan a legal case and claim against him and Israel in "The Supreme Court of Heaven".

Against him, and against Israel, Wow!

The question we must all ask ourselves: What accursed thing or things have our fathers and mothers brought into their homes and lives, which we are now reliving and repeating, and is a violation against the word and law of God, which the accuser is now using against us in "The Supreme Court of Heaven?

Achan violated the word and law of God when he hid forbidden items in his house.

Although this may be a difficult and uncomfortable concept to come to terms with, this question must be asked and answered if we are to be delivered and set free from all the accusations brought against us by Satan.

Achan took of that which was forbidden. He took the forbidden items and hid them in his house, by so doing he violated the word and law of God, this gave Satan, the accuser a legal case against him in "The Supreme Court of Heaven".

The devastating consequences of his action is recorded in Joshua 7:24-25

"And Joshua, and all Israel with him, took Achan the son of Zerah, and the silver and the garment, and the wedge of gold, and his sons, and his daughters, and his oxen, and his asses, and his sheep, and his tent and all that he had, and they brought them unto the valley of Achor." (v24)

The consequences of disobeying the commandments of God can be devastating.

"And Joshua said, why hast thou troubled us? The Lord shall trouble thee this day and all Israel stoned him with stones, and burned them with fire, after they had stoned them with stones." (v25)

What a tragic end. Why was Achan's story so extreme you may ask? Let's not forget what God had said in Joshua 6:18, *"And ye in any wise keep yourselves from the accused thing, lest ye make yourselves accursed, when ye take of the accursed thing and make the camp of Israel a curse and trouble it."*

The consequences of disobeying the commandments of God can be devastating; not only for the offender, but for all who are associated and in relationship with them.

Jericho had miraculously fallen, and although Israel was now in a place of blessings, yet because of one man's act of disobedience, God could not defend and protect them. The law of "The Supreme Court of Heaven" had been trespassed against; it had been violated and broken.

The consequence of which was the death and destruction of all that pertained to Achan. However, the consequences did not end there, because what was supposed to have been a relatively easy and sure victory for Israel when they fought against the city of Ai, turned out to be a battle which ended in death and defeat; thirty-six of Israel's soldiers were killed. Joshua 7:1-5

The accuser brought a legal case against Achan and Israel, and the Judge declared, "Guilty as charged."

> *In "The Supreme Court of Heaven" the accuser stands before the Judge with his case against you and me.*

Believers, in "The Supreme Court of Heaven" the accuser stands before the Judge with his case against you and me. His argument is, 'I have a legal case and right, based on the fact that their fathers and mothers have broken your commandments and their children are now doing the same things as did their parents.'

Satan therefore lays out his argument as to why he should be allowed to introduce into the people of God's families, things like:

- Sickness and pain
- Guilt and shame
- Lack and poverty
- Breakdowns and even premature deaths, etc.

This may all be true Satan, your argument against us is accurate, but there is something very important that you have failed to grasp in what you think is your water-tight argument and case; that is, that the God we serve is not just the Judge, He is also the Law-maker and the Law-giver.

He is the One who made the provision for the salvation of Rahab and her entire household. This provision and salvation was based on that extended scarlet thread and rope:

Our God who we serve is not just the Judge, He is also the Law-maker and the Law-giver.

- Abraham grabbed hold of that rope and received salvation.
- Israel grabbed hold of that rope and experienced deliverance from Egypt.
- The thief on the cross grabbed hold of that rope and received eternal life.

That rope has extended from one generation to another and it has finally reached our generation.

Look at this glorious promise in Galatians 3:6-7

"Even as Abraham believed God, and it accounted to him for righteousness." (v6)

"Know ye therefore that they which are of faith, the same are the children of Abraham." (v7)

So, Achan took of that which was forbidden and died. We and our fathers may have sinned, hence Satan's case against us, we have no earthly or natural defence against his argument and his case.

The only way out of this dilemma is to believe and rely on the ability of our Defence Lawyer, the Lord Jesus Christ.

This rope, this scarlet thread, this extension of the Blood of Jesus Christ, the Lamb of God, is the only means by which we may be forgiven and acquitted of the crime of sin and its devastating consequences, namely hell and eternal damnation.

> *The Blood of Jesus Christ, the Lamb of God, is the only means by which we may be forgiven and acquitted of the crime of sin.*

The example of Jesus our Lord's ability to deliver and set free, can be clearly seen in one question which He asked those who sought to ensnare Him based on the Law which forbade any work on the Sabbath day.

Luke 13:16, "And ought not this woman, being a daughter of Abraham whom Satan hath bound, lo, these eighteen years, be loosed from this bond on the Sabbath day?"

This woman, verse 11 tells us, had, *"...a spirit of infirmity eighteen years, and was bowed together, and could in no wise lift up herself."*

Was this scoliosis or curvature of the spine? Was it hereditary?

The source and cause of entry is unimportant, the consequence or result of the problem was that she, *"...could in no wise lift up herself."*

But what I want you to be aware of are the words of our Advocate, Intercessor and Defence Lawyer:

"And ought not this woman, being a daughter of Abraham whom Satan hath bound, lo these eighteen years, be loosed from this bond on the Sabbath day?" (Luke 13:16)

It is our birthright, as children of Abraham, to be delivered and set free from every accusation and attack of our adversary.

It is our birthright, as children of Abraham, to be delivered and set free from every accusation and attack of our adversary.

Chapter 8

Acts 16:13

"And on the Sabbath we went beyond the city gate to the riverside, where we had reason to believe there was a place for prayer..." (WNT)

It is stated that according to Jewish tradition a congregation was only constituted or recognised where there were at least ten households, with ten men as the head of each household, present.

This meant that without this, a synagogue could not be used, and prayer would have to be done elsewhere, preferably outdoors and by a riverside.

Upon entering Philippi and finding no synagogue, Paul joined a group of women by a riverside who were conducting a prayer meeting.

As previously mentioned, in order to gather in a synagogue, at least ten households, headed by ten men, had to be the minimum number present.

According to Jewish customs, in order to gather in a synagogue for worship, there had to be a minimum of ten households headed by ten men.

It was at this place that Lydia, the business woman was born again, but had they not been by the riverside there would have been no water to baptise her.

Unless we gather at a place of worship where the water is flowing, there will be no refreshing and there will be no Holy Spirit baptism.

The significance of the number ten can be seen in Genesis 18 and 19 which speaks about the destruction of Sodom and Gomorrah.

Having relayed to Abraham the reason for their visit, that being the total destruction of Sodom and Gomorrah, the heavenly beings who were sent by God from "The Supreme Court of Heaven", informed him of the impending judgement and doom.

The biblical significance of the number ten can be seen in Genesis chapters 18 and 19.

Two of the supernatural guests who visited Abraham were angels, the third visitor was the Lord Jesus himself. Genesis 13:1 says, *"And the LORD appeared to him..."* the word used for Lord here is "Jehovah" which means the self-existing one, the eternal one, the covenant keeping God.

This was a pre-incarnate manifestation of the Lord Jesus Christ.

The judgement was passed in "The Supreme Court of Heaven", yet note what happened next: *"And the men......turned their faces from thence and went toward Sodom, but Abraham stood yet before the Lord." (v22)*

Knowing the mercy and love of God, Abraham stepped into the role and office of an intercessor and stood in the gap and pleaded with the Judge, asking for mercy.

Between verses 24-32 we see him interceding to God, asking for pardon if there were 50 righteous people in the land. From fifty, he went all the way down to ten, where he stopped the intercession.

"And he said, O let not the Lord be angry and I will speak yet but this once: Peradventure ten shall be found there. And he said, I will not destroy it for ten's sake." (v32)

If we are going to seek the help of the Judge of all men, we must approach Him with awe and godly fear.

Note Abraham's cautious and reverent approach to God as he appealed on behalf of Sodom and Gomorrah. If we are going to stand before God in "The Supreme Court of Heaven", if we are going to seek the help of the Judge of all men, we must approach Him with awe and godly fear because He is a consuming fire.

He is holy and righteous and we are not. We must understand that it is only because of His love and mercy that we are not consumed.

So why did Abraham stop the intercession and negotiations at ten?

As previously mentioned, the requirement for a synagogue gathering was ten households headed by ten men, where the number of ten was not present, there could be no synagogue gathering.

Abraham knew, as he had stated in verse 25, *"...Shall not the judge of all the earth do right?"*

His judgement is complete and just, and as such, there was no further room for negotiations. So verse 33 concludes, *"And the LORD went His way..."*

Ten is one of God's perfect numbers; it signifies that which is complete and whole:

> *Number ten is one of God's perfect numbers which signifies that which is whole and Complete.*

- It is the number of the Ten Commandments.
- It is the number of the tithes.
- It is the number of testing, for example, it was ten spies who brought back an evil report of the promised land.

Exodus 12:3 declares, *"Speak ye unto all the congregation of Israel saying, In the tenth day of this month they shall take to them every man a lamb according to the house of their father's, a lamb for an house."*

A sentence had been passed, judgement was coming and the only means of escape was the applied blood on the tenth day of the month.

Ten was the Jewish month of "Tebeth" and it was in that month that Esther was taken into the house of King Ahaseuerus (Esther 2:16)

According to Genesis 18:1, the dialogue between Abraham and the heavenly beings began with him sitting in the doorway of his tent, and concluded with the angels travelling to Sodom where they met Lot, who was sitting at the gate of Sodom.

It was also at the gate of the city that Boaz sat while conducting business with his kinsmen concerning the land in Ruth 4:1-3.

Ten was the Jewish month of "Tebeth" and it was in that month that Esther was taken into the house of king Ahaseuerus.

Like Abraham who pleaded for Sodom where his nephew Lot lived, may all of our family members who are living in a wrong place spiritually, find grace and mercy, may they be saved and find forgiveness, in the name of Jesus Christ, our Intercessor and Advocate in "The Supreme Court of Heaven".

Chapter 9

1 John 2:1-2

"My little children, these things write I unto you, that ye sin not. And if any man sin, we have an advocate with the Father; Jesus Christ the righteous." (v1)

"And He is the propitiation for our sins, and not for ours only, but also for the sins of the whole world." (v2)

John previously said in 1 John 1:8-10

"If we say that we have no sin, we deceive ourselves, and the truth is not in us." (v8)

"If we confess our sins, he is faithful and just to forgive us our sins and to cleanse us from all unrighteousness." (v9)

"If we say that we have not sinned, we make him a liar and his word is not in us." (v10)

In these three verses, the apostle John talks to us about two aspects of sin:

1. Our nature of sin:

This is what he is referring to in verse 8 where he says, *"If we say that we have no sin, we deceive ourselves and the truth is not in us."*

John is not speaking about habitual or wilful sins here, he is speaking about man's nature of sin, otherwise known as the Adamic or fallen nature.

2. Individual and personal sins committed:

This is what he is speaking about in verse 10 where he says, *"If we say that we have not sinned, we make Him a liar and His word is not in us."*

The nature of man is sinful and as such his natural inclination is to sin and do that which is contrary to the will and word of God.

I want to make something absolutely crystal clear here, it is a gross mistake to downplay or undermine the awfulness of sin and its consequences; the punishment for sin is death, make no mistake about that.

> *It is a gross mistake to downplay the awfulness of sin and its consequences. The consequences of sin is death.*

God hates sin. His judgement and wrath against sin is severe and still stands today. The Bible says, *"The wages of sin is death." (Rom 6:23).* This will not change because it is not popular in today's world of liberation and modern thinking; sin has devastating consequences.

The word "confess" used in 1 John 1:9 means to agree with, to acknowledge.

We must agree with, and acknowledge the fact that our natural tendency is to sin; we do not have to make an effort to sin, it is man's default setting.

The apostle Paul understood what John wrote about here, listen to his words in Romans 7:22-25

"For I delight in the law of God after the inward man." (v22)

"But I see another law in my members, warring against the law of my mind and bringing me into captivity to the law of sin which is in my members." (v23)

"O wretched man that I am! who shall deliver me from the body of this death?" (v24)

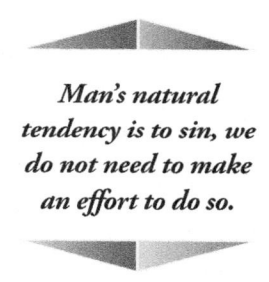

Man's natural tendency is to sin, we do not need to make an effort to do so.

"I thank God through Jesus Christ our Lord. So then with the mind I myself serve the law of God, but with the flesh the law of sin." (v25)

What a dilemma, what a dichotomy!

1 John 2:1, *"My little children, these things write I unto you, that ye sin not. And if any man sin, we have an advocate with the Father, Jesus Christ the righteous."*

"My little children..." John speaks to us as a tender, loving father. A father who knows that his children are inexperienced and as such are at a disadvantage and are in danger. We can be misled, manipulated and led or tricked into doing that which is wrong.

In spite of our failings, shortcomings and sins, John tells us that God is faithful and just to forgive us our sins and to cleanse us from all unrighteousness.

How can God forgive and cleanse us from all sins?

"We have an advocate with the Father, Jesus Christ the righteous."

What a glorious provision! This, my friend is the only way that we can be forgiven and cleansed from all sins. Look at those words again, *"We have an advocate with the Father.."*

> *We have an advocate who pleads our cause before the Father and Judge in the Supreme Court of Heaven.*

The Greek word "Parakle-tos" means, advocate, an intercessor, one who consoles, comforts.

We have One who stands in "The Supreme Court of Heaven" on our behalf, what does He do for us, the believers?

- He pleads the believers cause before the Father and Judge.
- He stands as an intermediary between justice and mercy for those who believe and have been forgiven of their sins.

1 John 2:2, *"And He is the propitiation for our sins, and not for ours only, but also for the sins of the whole world."*

The word propitiation is an interesting word, it comes from the Greek word "Hilas-mos" which means, atonement, expiation.

To expiate is to mend or repair that which is broken, to redo or remake.

Jesus the righteous, is both our Propitiator and our Expiator.

> *Jesus the righteous, is both our Propitiator and our Expiator.*

Listen to the words of our Propitiator and Expiator, John 14:30, *"Hereafter I will not talk much with you, for the prince of this world cometh and hath nothing in me."*

Satan the accuser and prince of this world cometh, but he has nothing, no power, no authority over me, says Jesus the righteous.

You and I cannot say that, the truth is: Psalms 130:3-4

"If thou, LORD shouldest mark iniquity, O Lord, who shall stand?" (v3)

"But there is forgiveness with thee, that thou mayest be feared." (v4)

1 John 4:10, *"Herein is love, not that we loved God, but that he loved us, and sent his Son to be the propitiation for our sins."*

The shedding of Jesus' blood and giving of His life on Calvary gives the repentant sinner an audience with the Judge in "The Supreme Court of Heaven". The blood of Jesus is our ultimate defence; it is the blood that silences the accuser's voice.

> **The blood of Jesus is our ultimate defence; it is the blood that silences the accuser's voice.**

Romans 3:24-26

"Being justified freely by his grace through the redemption that is in Christ Jesus." (v24)

"Whom God hath set forth to be a propitiation through faith in his blood, to declare his righteousness for the remission of sins that are past, through the forbearance of God." (v25)

"To declare, I say at this time his righteousness, that he might be just and the justifier of him which believeth in Jesus." (v26)

This is wonderful news for the believer! We are redeemed, forgiven and brought back from Satan's prison of sin, by the propitiation and atoning work of Jesus our Expiator to His glorious name be all glory and praise.

He is justified by virtue of what He has done and He is the one who justifies us who believe in His name.

Chapter 10

Hebrews 12:18-25

"For ye are not come unto the mount that might be touched, and that burned with fire, nor unto blackness, and darkness, and tempest." (v18)

"And the sound of a trumpet, and the voice of words, which voice they that heard entreated that the word should not be spoken to them anymore." (v19)

"For they could not endure that which was commanded, and if so much as a beast touch the mountain, it shall be stoned or thrust through with a dart." (v20)

"And so terrible was the sight, that Moses said, I exceedingly fear and quake." (v21)

"But ye are come unto mount Sion and unto the city of the living God, the heavenly Jerusalem, and to an innumerable company of angels" (v22)

"To the general assembly and the Church of the firstborn, which are written in heaven and to God the Judge of all, and to the spirits of just men made perfect" (v23)

"And to Jesus the mediator of the new covenant, and to the blood of sprinkling, that speaketh better things than that of Abel." (v24)

"See that ye refuse not Him that speaketh. For if they escaped not who refused him that spake on earth, much more shall not we escape, if we turn away from him that speaketh from heaven." (v25)

Israel, under the Law and Old Covenant, saw the glory and power of God at Mount Sinai.

Under the old order animals became the substitute and sacrifice for man's sin but animals are not humans, and as such, no animal could ever be a perfect and viable substitute or sacrifice for the sins of mankind.

In His humanity, Jesus our Lord became what no animal could be, He became the perfect sacrifice for sin; this is known as the New Covenant.

Under the old order the place where God was approached by man was physical, not spiritual and because of his fallen nature, it was a terrifying experience for man.

> **Man simply does not qualify to have a hearing with the righteous Judge.**

Therefore, any and all attempts to approach God from a humanistic and earthly standpoint will fail; the individual who tries to do so will experience the judgement and wrath of God.

Man of himself does not qualify to have a hearing with the righteous Judge.

He cannot go up to heaven to plead his case, yet in His tender loving mercy, God came down to earth to meet fallen man.

The verses highlighted in Hebrews 12 have to be among the most sublime texts in the Bible. It peels back the curtain and veil of the supernatural and gives us a glimpse into the heavenly realm and what really happens when believers truly gather together to worship their God.

In His tender loving mercy, God came down to earth to meet fallen man.

For the believers, we do not come to the mount that can be touched and burns with fire, blackness, darkness and tempest.

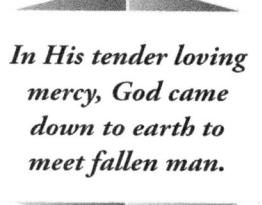

- Fire symbolises the holiness and righteousness of God.
- Blackness and darkness speaks of the God who is hidden from the sight of men, where there is blackness and darkness all we can see are shadows of that which is real and tangible.
- Tempest symbolises the fierceness and judgement of God's wrath against sin.

If we try to appropriate the presence of God the Judge, based on our own righteousness and works, all we will experience is judgement and condemnation.

Romans 3:19-20

"Now we know that what things soever the law saith, it saith to them who it saith to them who are under the law; that every mouth may be stopped and all the world may become guilty before God." (v19)

"Therefore by the deeds of the law there shall no flesh be justified in his sight; for by the law is the knowledge of sin." (v20)

Mount Sinai, the place where the Law was first given, is physical and earthly, we do not gather there to worship our God; we gather at mount Sion and unto the city of the living God, the heavenly Jerusalem, and to an innumerable company of angels.

Although Mount Sion is not physical, by faith the believer can go there and have an audience with the Judge in "The Supreme Court of Heaven".

You may be thinking, how is that possible? Well, we have a man who came down from "The Supreme Court of Heaven". He came down that we may go up.

We can rejoice and praise our God, who has made the provision for those who believe, to have an audience with Him. This He has done through the ability of our Advocate and Intercessor.

Whenever we go up to "The Supreme Court of Heaven" by faith, we have a man who stands by our side and pleads our cause, His name is Jesus Christ the righteous.

Whenever we go up to the Supreme Court of Heaven by faith, we have audience with our Heavenly Father through the ability of our Advocate and Intercessor - Jesus.

We are come unto Mount Sion, not Mount Sinai, what is the difference?

- Mount Sinai is where the Law was given, the word Sinai means, thorn. For those who are in sin, the Commandments and Laws of God are thorny and punitive.

- Mount Sion is the abode of God, the word Sion means, Church, it means militant and triumphant.

My goodness, the Church, the Ecclesia of God is supposed to be a place where Jehovah abides, it is meant to be militant and triumphant!

The Church is supposed to be uncompromising, glorious and powerful. We are meant to be an army which is moving forward, conquering and taking territory. When we speak the words of the General, hell and all of its demons should shake and quiver in terror because we are filled with the Holy Spirit and He has given an order for the Christians to turn their world upside down.

The Church is the Ecclesia of God where Jehovah abides, we ought to be militant and triumphant.

Hebrews 12:22-23

"But ye are come unto mount Sion and unto the city of the living God, the heavenly Jerusalem, and to an innumerable company of angels," (v22)

"To the general assembly and the church of the firstborn, which are written in heaven, and to God the Judge of all, and to the spirits of just men made perfect." (v23)

In the Old Testament they would have convocation once a year, today we have convocations or conventions once a year, but none of their gatherings and none of our gatherings can be compared to *"The general assembly and church of the firstborn."*

Jesus is the Firstborn, He is the founder and beginner of the Church, He is the very source and life of the Church.

Note who is gathered in this incredible assembly *"...An innumerable company of angels...spirits of just men made perfect."*

> *Jesus is the Firstborn, He is the founder and beginner of the Church, He is the very source and life of the Church.*

Just men made perfect are those who have died in Christ and are no longer subjected to this world of pain, sin and decay; they are perfectly delivered and set free.

Then Hebrews 12:24 tells us of another who is a part of this assembly, *"And to Jesus the mediator of the new covenant, and to the blood of sprinkling, that spaketh better things than that of Abel."*

The blood of Abel cries out for justice. The Blood of Jesus is far superior, it does not focus on the injustice that was done.

No, it offers forgiveness and mercy.

That sprinkled blood is all cleansing; it is the only way to be atoned and receive forgiveness and justification.

It is not only our life source, it is also our means of defence and protection from the attacks and onslaughts of our enemies. Praise be to God who has given us His Only Begotten, the Firstborn, so that we, through His Blood, can be sons of God.

Chapter 11

2 Kings 19:14-17

"And Hezekiah received the letter of the hand of the messengers, and read it, and Hezekiah went up into the house of the LORD and spread it before the LORD." (v14)

"And Hezekiah prayed before the LORD, and said, O LORD God of Israel which dwellest between the cherubims, thou art the God, even thou alone, of all the kingdoms of the earth thou hast made heaven and earth." (v15)

"LORD, bow down thine ear and hear, open LORD thine eyes, and see, and hear the words of Sennacherib, which hath sent him to reproach the living God." (v16)

"Of a truth LORD, the kings of Assyria have destroyed the nations and their lands." (v17)

The Assyrian's were known for their military might and strength; they overcame and conquered all who stood against them.

Sennacherib, their king, had a chief prince by the name of Rabshakeh, who was very vocal, arrogant and self-assured.

He said in 2Kings 18:20, *"Thou sayest, (but they are vain words,) I have counsel and strength for the war. Now on whom doest thou trust, that thou rebellest against me?"*

He therefore wrote a threatening letter to Hezekiah, the king of Judah, in which he reminded him of the fact that Sennacherib and his mighty Assyrian army had overpowered and destroyed every opposing army and nation that stood against them.

This was a very distressing and disturbing message sent by the hand of the enemy of God's people.

Hezekiah's response:

"And Hezekiah received the letter of the hand of the messengers, and read it, and Hezekiah went up into the house of the LORD, and spread it before the LORD." (v14)

> **King Hezekiah received a very distressing and disturbing message sent by the hand of the enemy of God's people.**

The word used for house here is "Bah-yith" which means, house, temple or court.

Once Hezekiah had read and understood the content of Sennacherib's letter, he took it into the house of the Lord and spread it before the Him.

Reading the content of your enemy's letter, will reveal the magnitude of the threat and as such will cause worry and fear.

In going up into the house of the Lord with the letter and spreading it before the Lord, Hezekiah was demonstrating his recognition of the fact that this problem was too big for him or his people to handle.

If you want the Lord to help and intervene in the problems which confront you, once you understand the nature and content of the devil's plans, it is wise to go up to "The Supreme Court of Heaven" and spread the letter before the Judge.

Note Hezekiah's words in verse 16, *"LORD, bow down thine ear and hear, open LORD thine eyes, and see, and hear the words of Sennacherib, which hath sent him to reproach the living God."*

Although Sennacherib had picked a fight against Hezekiah and Judah, Hezekiah recognised that both Judah and Jerusalem belonged to God. He was therefore right when he said that it is against you, the living God that our enemies have come against.

> *It is wise to go up to the Supreme Court of Heaven, if you want the Lord to help and intervene in the problems which confront you.*

No wonder Zechariah declared in Zechariah 2:8, *"For thus saith the LORD of hosts, After the glory hath He sent me unto the nations which spoiled you, for He that toucheth you toucheth the apple of His eyes."*

"The LORD of glory has sent me against the nations that oppress you, for he who harms you sticks His finger in Jehovah's eye." (TAY)

Believers, the battle is not yours or mine, it is the Lords and He is the Lord of hosts. If we go up to "The Supreme Court of Heaven" and hand over the letter from our enemies to the Judge and great I Am, He will send His mighty angels who will fight for and defend us.

Sennacherib and his mighty army, consisting of 185 thousand men, surrounded Jerusalem, but what they did not know was the fact that Hezekiah, *"...went up into the house of the LORD and spread the letter before the LORD"*, who was now on the case.

> *Believers, the battle is not yours or mine, it is the Lords and He is the Lord of hosts.*

The Judge despatched an army of His elite invisible soldiers, who came down from heaven to earth. In the natural Jerusalem was surrounded, but so also were the Assyrian soldiers, even more-so in fact. What do I mean?

Psalms 125:2, *"As the mountains are round about Jerusalem, so the LORD is round about His people from henceforth, even for ever."*

Still don't understand what I am saying?

When the Syrian army came against Israel in 2 Kings 6, verse 17 tells us, "And Elisha prayed, and said, Lord I pray thee, open his eyes that he may see. And the LORD opened the eyes of the young man, and he saw, and behold the mountain was full of horses and chariots of fire round about Elisha."

> *To see what is happening behind the scenes and into the supernatural requires revelation and illumination.*

Although in the same geographical location, what Elisha was seeing was very different from what his servant was seeing. To see what is happening behind the scenes and into the supernatural requires revelation and illumination.

Elisha had it, but he could not give it. This can only come from God Himself. We must therefore pray, "Lord open my eyes that I may see."

God's declaration concerning Sennacherib and his army:

2Kings 19:32, *"Therefore thus saith the LORD concerning the king of Assyria, He shall not come into this city, nor shoot an arrow there, nor come before it with shield, nor cast a bank against it."*

This will be the case because, *"For I will defend this city to save it for mine own sake, and for my servant David's sake." (v34)*

God said He would defend Jerusalem because of two reasons:

- For mine own sake.
- For my servant David's sake.

Was God going to save Jerusalem because David was a great king? Was He going to save it because David was a worshipper?

Oh no. The opening words from the first book of the New Testament reads:

"The book of the generation of Jesus Christ, the son of David, the son of Abraham." (Matt 1:1)

> *God saved Jerusalem because of two reasons: For the sake of His name and for His servant David's sake.*

Micah 5:2, *"But thou, Bethlehem Ephratah, though thou be little among the thousands of Judah, yet out of thee shall He come forth unto me that is to be ruler in Israel, whose goings forth have been from of old, from everlasting."*

"Whose goings forth have been from of old, from everlasting."

This is speaking about the Son and offspring of David, who would later declare in John 8:58, *"...before Abraham was, I am."*

Neither Abraham nor David could be describes as being "from everlasting." Jesus even said, *"...before Abraham was (past) I am (present)."*

The Lord God Almighty had predetermined before time began, that His Son, the Lord Jesus Christ would come through the Davidic lineage, because of what He had determined and because of His prophetic purpose, *"...I will defend this city to save it for mine own sake and for my servant David's sake."*

The outcome for the Assyrian army:

"And it came to pass that night, that the angel of the LORD went out, and smote in the camp of the Assyrians, an hundred four score and five thousand, and when they arose early in the morning, behold, they were all dead corpses." (2Kings 19:35)

Almighty God had predetermined before time began, that His Son Jesus Christ would come through David's Lineage.

This is funny, because dead people do not rise in the morning. What the verse is saying is that Judah, for whom death would have certainly been their fate, because Hezekiah their king went up to the house of the Lord with the problem, a judgement was made against Israel's enemies in "The Supreme Court of Heaven" and a sentence of death was given to all the Assyrian army.

Judah went to bed on that fateful night, having trepidation and fear in their hearts, but when they awoke in the morning light, to their amazement, all of the Assyrian soldiers were dead.

185 thousand soldiers were slain by the army of Almighty God. I don't know what you are facing today, I don't know who has risen up against you but can I suggest that you do what Hezekiah did.

"And Hezekiah went up into the house of the Lord and spread it (the problem) before the Lord."

When confronted with accusations and threats from your enemy the devil and accuser of the brethren, it is best to take the situation and problem to "The Supreme Court of Heaven". There the Lord your Defender, will defend and protect you.

Chapter 12

Ephesians 2:4-6

"But God, who is rich in mercy, for His great love wherewith He loved us"(v4)

"Even when we were dead in sins, hath quickened us together with Christ, (by grace ye are saved)" (v5)

"And hath raised us up together and made us sit together in heavenly places in Christ Jesus." (v6)

The term "heavenly places" is only recorded or mentioned in Ephesians where it is repeated four times; 1:3, 1:20, 2:6 and 3:10

> *The book of Ephesians is the New Testament counterpart of the Old Testament book of Joshua.*

The book of Ephesians is the New Testament counterpart of the Old Testament book of Joshua, which is primarily about the possession of the Promised Land.

Other renderings of the term "heavenly places":

- *"…And has raised us with Him, from the dead and enthroned us with Him, in the heavenly realm" (WNT).*
- *"And has lifted us right out of the old life to take our place with him in Christ in the Heavens" (PHILLIPS)*

Although we remain flesh and blood after we are born-again, and although we live in a physical world and reside on a planet called earth, we must understand that as believers and followers of the Lord Jesus Christ, we are actually also citizens of another world and country.

God the Father has given us a new nature, which gives us a new identity. Believers, we are now "Sons of God" and we are, right now, sitting together with Jesus our Lord, in the realms of heaven.

The resurrection of Jesus Christ from the dead was a demonstration of God's incredible power.

The resurrection of Jesus Christ from the dead was a demonstration of God's incredible power.

It is also evidence of what Father God can and will do for all those who are seated in the heavens with His beloved and dear Son.

Jesus was not only raised from the dead, by which He conquered sin, death and hell, He was also given an exalted position of absolute authority, dominion and power and is seated at the right-hand of God the Father.

This is in fulfilment of Psalms 110:1, *"The LORD said unto my Lord, sit thou at my right-hand until I make thine enemies thy footstool."*

- The word used for the first reference to Lord, is Jehovah, which means the eternal, self-existing one.
- The word used for the second reference to Lord is, Adoni, which means master, controller, owner.

God the Father said to God the Son, *"Sit thou at my right-hand until I make thine enemies thy footstool."*

Sit thou at my right-hand until the time appointed when every knee must bow and every tongue will confess that you are "Adoni" master, controller and owner of everything.

Our Lord's exalted position and what it means for the believer is highlighted in Ephesians 1:17-23

> **God the Father said to God the Son "Sit at my right hand until I make your enemies your footstool"**

"That the God of our Lord Jesus Christ, the Father of glory, may give unto you the spirit of wisdom and revelation in the knowledge of him." (v17)

"The eyes of your understanding being enlightened; that ye may know what is the hope of his calling, and what the riches of the glory of his inheritance in the saints," (v18)

"And what is the exceeding greatness of his power to us-ward who believe, according to the working of his mighty power," (v19)

"Which he wrought in Christ, when he raised him from the dead, and set him at his own right-hand, in the heavenly places," (v20)

"Far above all principality and power, and might, and dominion, and every name that is named, not only in this world, but also in that which is to come," (v21)

"And hath put all things under his feet, and gave him to be the head over all things to the church," (v22)

THE SUPREME COURT OF HEAVEN

"Which is his body, the fulness of him that filleth all in all." (v23)

"And has appointed him universal and supreme head of the Church." (WNT)

Goes on to say, *"And in the body lives fully the one who fills the whole universe." (PHILLIPS)*

> **The Lord has invested His power in those who are born-again and filled with His Holy Spirit.**

In verse 19 Paul uses the word, exceeding, which comes from the Greek word "Hup-er-ballon" which means; surpassing, unlimited, beyond comprehension or imagination.

He also uses the word, greatness, from "Meg-thos" meaning; mighty and explosive. It is from this word that we get the English words megaton and mega. We are talking about extreme and explosive power here. This is no ordinary power.

It is above and beyond that which can be called ordinary or normal. It is God's supernatural and dynamic power of which nothing in this world can be compared.

All of this, Paul says, is to us-ward!

May the Lord our God help us to really understand who we are in Christ. We are actually God's inheritance, and He wants returns on that which He has invested in us. Our God wants us to experience His "Meg-thos".

Paul says, *"I want you to know what is the riches of the glory of his inheritance."* He has invested power in those who are born-again and filled with His Holy Spirit; the paraclete in us is incredibly dynamic and explosive.

Satan the accuser, is so foolish in his attempt to discredit and disqualify us from the blessings and the inheritance which is ours. He brings us before "The Supreme Court of Heaven" but what he does not seem to understand is this:

"And hath raised us up together and made us sit together, in heavenly places, in Christ Jesus." (Eph 2:6)

Look at that:

- And hath
- Raised us up
- Made us sit together.

Hath – Raised – Made, all past tense, they have already happened.

Made us sit together? Sit together where? In the realms of heaven.

"...And has raised us up with Him, from the dead and enthroned us with Him, in the heavenly realms." (WNT)

"And has lifted us right out of the old life to take our place with Him, in Christ Jesus, in the heavens." (PHILLIPS)

The apostle Paul prayed that God the Father would give us wisdom and revelation in the knowledge of Him, Jesus. He also prayed that the eyes of our understanding would be enlightened that we may know. Without this we will not be able to be the people of God we are supposed to be in this world.

> **Apostle Paul prayed that the eyes of our understanding be enlightened that we may know; without this we are unable to be the people of God we ought to be in this world.**

Because God has already raised us up, and made us to sit together in the realms of heaven, and because Jesus our Lord and Advocate stands with us, I therefore declare and decree:

Satan, before you came here with your voice of accusation, we were already here. Before you gathered your evidence against us, we were already set free and acquitted, because Jesus has paid the price for our forgiveness, justification and acquittal.

Chapter 13

Daniel 10:11-14

"And he said unto me, O Daniel, a man greatly beloved, understand the words that I speak unto thee, and stand upright, for unto thee am I now sent. And when he had spoken this word unto me, I stood trembling." (v11)

"Then said he unto me, Fear not Daniel, for from the first day that thou didst set thine heart to understand, and to chasten thyself before thy God, thy words were heard, and I am come for thy words." (v12)

"But the prince of the kingdom of Persia withstood me one and twenty days, but lo, Michael, one of the chief princes, came to help me, and I remained there with the kings of Persia." (v13)

"Now I am come to make thee understand what shall befall thy people in the latter days, for yet the vision is for many days." (v14)

In many ways what we are seeing here in Daniel 10, is similar to Ezekiel's vision in which he was given a glimpse into the heavens.

"Now it came to pass in the thirteenth year, in the fourth month, in the fifth day of the month, as I was among the captives by the river of Chebar, that the heavens were opened, and I saw visions of God." (Eze 1:1)

John also had a similar experience in Revelation 1:17 he says, *"And when I saw him, I fell at his feet as dead. And he laid his right hand upon me saying unto me, Fear not; I am the first and the last."*

Upon meeting the angel Daniel said in 10:8, *"...there remaineth no strength in me..."* he also fell to the ground in absolute fear and terror.

Flesh and blood will always be struck with fear, whenever it comes into contact with the supernatural and celestial beings. The angel therefore alleviated Daniel's fear by declaring in verse 12, *"...Fear not..."*

In verse 11 it says, *"And he said unto me, O Daniel, a man greatly beloved, understand the words that I speak unto thee..."*

> **Flesh and blood will always be struck with fear, whenever it comes into contact with the supernatural and celestial beings.**

There is no doubting the fact that God loves all men (John 3:16). However, there are those who, by virtue of their calling and willingness to seek after God, have experienced a unique relationship with Him; which gives them a deeper and closer insight as to who God really is.

For example men like; Enoch, Abraham, Joseph, Daniel and John the Baptist!

The angel informed Daniel that the purpose for his visit was because of his words, *"...I am come for thy words." (v12)*

So, you do not think the words you speak are relevant, that they have no consequence in your life? I want you to know that your words either invite and employ the service of angels, or demons.

In fact, the angel said, *"...from the first day that thou didst set thine heart to understand and to chasten thyself before thy God, thy words were heard."*

The angel who came because of Daniel's words, went on to tell him something which is alarming and quite disturbing. He said that he had been withstood for twenty-one days by the prince of the kingdom of Persia! (V13)

> **The angel of the Lord informed Daniel that the purpose for his visit was because of his words.**

Wait a minute, how long did Daniel pray for? *"In those days, I Daniel was mourning three full weeks." (Dan 10:2)*

Daniel prayed for three full weeks and from the very first day of his prayer meeting, God answered his prayer and dispatched an angel from "The Supreme Court of Heaven".

But the angel, and the answer to Daniel's request was held-up; the angel encountered turbulence and resistance from the prince of the kingdom of Persia.

This prince could not have been a human being, because the conflict and battle did not occur on the earth, it took place in the realm of the heavens.

The prince was a spiritual strongman, a satanic official who was given authority over the realm of Persia. His authority ranged from governmental, economic, religious and social authority. He had total control of the affairs of the citizens of Persia.

> *The angel of the Lord encountered turbulence and resistance from the prince of the kingdom of Persia.*

The angel which came from "The Supreme Court of Heaven" was sent in response to Daniel's twenty-one days of fasting and prayer. Daniel's request was in conjunction with God's prophetic word.

"In the first year of his reign (Darius) I Daniel understood by books the number of the years, whereof the word of the LORD came to Jeremiah the prophet, that he would accomplish seventy years in the desolation of Jerusalem." (Dan 9:2)

Then verse 21 goes on to say, *"Yea, while I was speaking in prayer, even the man Gabriel, whom I had seen in the vision at the beginning, being caused to fly swiftly, touched me about the time of the evening oblation."*

In spite of the fact that this angel was sent by God from "The Supreme Court of Heaven", yet still we read these astonishing words in Daniel 10:13, *"But the prince of the kingdom of Persia withstood me..."*

The warfare and resistance were intense and severe. So much so in fact, that God had to send reinforcement in the person of Michael, one of heaven's chief angels, who helped in the struggle.

This is the first time that the angel Michael's name is mentioned in the Bible. He is also mentioned twice more in the book of Daniel, in 10:21 and 12:1.

Listen very carefully, although Michael was a higher-ranking angel than the devil, Jude tells us something very interesting:

"Yet Michael the archangel, when contending with the devil, he disputed about the body of Moses, durst not bring against him a railing accusation, but said, The Lord rebuke thee." (Jude 1:9)

> *The Lord had to send Michael, one of heaven's chief angels as reinforcement because the warfare and resistance by the spirit prince over Persia was intense and severe.*

Michael refused to be drawn into a discussion or slanging match with Satan, who is a slanderer and accuser. Instead of arguing, Michael left judgement to the Judge of all, knowing that in "The Supreme Court of Heaven" Satan had already been tried, found guilty and sentenced.

He therefore simply said, *"The Lord rebuke thee."*

Satan you are trying to stop the plan of God for my life; you have set-up opposition and resistance over my territory.

But listen, Zechariah 3:2, *"And the Lord said unto Satan, The LORD rebuke thee, O Satan, even the LORD that hath chosen Jerusalem rebuke thee, is not this a brand plucked out of the fire?"*

In the same way that God plucked Joshua and Judah out of the fire of Babylonian captivity, He also plucked His beloved Son Jesus Christ out of the fire of the crucifixion and death.

I want you to know, Satan, when you accuse and resist me, that I am a brand who has been plucked out of the fire of sin and death.

Believers, through the blood of Jesus, we have been plucked out of the fire of sin and death.

Like Zechariah and Jude, I therefore say to you, *"The Lord rebuke you!"*

Chapter 14

Job 1:6 and 2:1

"Now there was a day when the sons of God came to present themselves before the LORD, and Satan came also among them." (Job 1:6)

"Again there was a day when the sons of God came to present themselves before the LORD, and Satan came also among them to present himself before the Lord." (Job 2:1)

Sons of God, as mentioned here, are actually angels or celestial beings, who were created by Elohim, the great God of Creation; they were created to serve Him.

Psalms 103:20-21

"Bless the Lord, ye his angels that excel in strength, that do his commandments, hearkening unto the voice of his word." (v20)

"Bless ye the Lord, all ye his hosts, ye ministers of his, that do his pleasure." (v21)

Job 1:6 and 2:1 speak to us about a gathering wherein the sons of God (angels) presented themselves before their maker and creator. This gathering is like that of an AGM, which is a time when managers give account of the performance of their various departments to the chairman of the company.

THE SUPREME COURT OF HEAVEN

A glimpse of the awesomeness of "The Supreme Court of Heaven" and the glory of the Lord God Almighty can be seen in Daniel 7:9-10.

"I beheld till the thrones were cast down, and the Ancient of days did sit, whose garment was white as snow, and the hair of his head like the pure wool, his throne was like the fiery flame, and His wheels like as burning fire." (v9)

"A fire stream issued and came forth from before him, thousand thousands ministered unto him, and ten thousand times ten thousand stood before him, the judgement was set, and the books were opened." (v10)

In the book of Job, we read that as the sons of God came to present themselves before God, Satan the accuser, also came among them.

The awesomeness of this scene is mind boggling and at the very least there are billions of angels represented here. Absolutely staggering!

As the sons of God came to present themselves before God, Satan the accuser, also came among them.

The Lord asked him in Job 1:7, *"...Whence comest thou...?"* Satan answered, *"...From going to and fro in the earth, and from walking up and down in it."*

The Lord, knowing what Satan's motive was in joining this gathering asked him, *"...Hast thou considered my servant Job...?" (v8)*

This question needs to be understood as God really saying, I know why you are here; you want permission to attack my servant Job.

Satan came to this celestial courtroom, in rage and anger at God, because He had blessed and shielded Job, and would not allow Satan access to him.

Satan's opening argument: 'Of course Job will serve you God. I mean, look at how much you have blessed him. Who would not serve you after being so favoured? I mean, you have built a hedge of protection around this man.'

> *Satan came to this celestial courtroom, in rage and anger at God, because He had blessed and shielded Job, and would not allow Satan access to him.*

There are two important lessons we must learn from this:

- Satan has to ask permission of the Judge before he can get to us.
- His ability to cause harm to God's people is limited.

Having received permission from the Judge, Job 1:12 and 2:7 both tell us that *"...Satan went forth from the presence of the Lord."*

The only time that Satan is given a hearing in "The Supreme Court of Heaven" is when it has to do with his attempt at accusing the believer.

After leaving the presence of God, Satan immediately turned his attention to Job, attacking him and all that he had, but after failing to cause Job to curse God, he then attacked his person, with sickness.

Job 1:21-22 shows us the character of the man.

"And said, Naked came I out of my mother's womb, and naked shall I return thither, the LORD gave and the LORD hath taken away, blessed be the name of the LORD." (v21)

"In all this Job sinned not, nor charged God foolishly." (v22)

Though Satan attacked Job and all that he had, he failed to get Job to deny and curse God.

These two verses validate Job 1:1, *"There was a man in the land of Uz, whose name was Job and that man was perfect and upright and one that feared God and eschewed evil."*

In his first attack against Job, Satan destroyed all of Job's earthly possessions, including his very own sons and daughters. His attempt was futile, he failed to get Job to deny and curse God.

We further read in Job 2:1, *"Again there was a day when the sons of God came to present themselves before the LORD and Satan came also among them to present himself before the LORD."*

This is actually a repeat of Job 1:6-8 except on this occasion, the Judge vindicates the accused and says of him in Job 2:3, *"…a perfect and upright man, one that feareth God and escheweth evil and still he holdeth fast his integrity, although thou movedst me against him, to destroy him without a cause."*

Satan then turned his attention to Job himself and afflicted him with boils and sickness. Again, Satan failed in his attempt to get Job to turn against his God.

It is important to realise that at no time was Job made aware of the fact that what he was experiencing and going through was the direct result of what was going on beyond and behind the veil of the natural and the visible.

Believers, the unusual trials, difficulties and hardships are as a result of the decisions which are made in the Supreme Court of Heaven.

This was all the result of a judgement that was made and passed in "The Supreme Court of Heaven".

Believers, what you are going through on the earth, those unusual and inexplicable trials, difficulties and hardships, are the result of decisions which are made in "The Supreme Court of Heaven".

The devil tried to accuse Job and prove to God that the only reason why Job was being faithful and serving Him was because He had blessed, protected and shielded him.

God therefore removed the hedge of protection and allowed the devil to attack him.

Job overcame the test, proved that not every man can be bought and stayed faithful to his God.

THE SUPREME COURT OF HEAVEN

Paul's experience of "The Supreme Court of Heaven"

"I knew a man in Christ, above fourteen years ago, whether in the body, I cannot tell, God knoweth, such an one caught up to the third heaven." 2 Cor 12:2)

Please understand this, the subject we are discussing, "The Supreme Court of Heaven", has nothing to do with our senses. It is not something logical or natural, it is spiritual. It is not an explanation, it is more an experience and as such, unless you are of the Spirit you will not be able to come to terms with what is outlined in this book.

The great apostle Paul said, his experience took place some fourteen years previously and that seems to be the only thing that he could rationally explain. He went on to say, *"...whether in the body I cannot tell, God knoweth...caught up into the third heaven."*

My friends, going up to "The Supreme Court of Heaven" requires us to move up to a higher place in God.

It requires moving beyond the realm of 'Churchism', customs and traditions.

Job 42:10 and 12 gives the believer God's perspective as to why He allows the accuser to attack them.

"And the Lord turned the captivity of Job, when he prayed for his friends, also the Lord gave Job twice as much as he had before." (v10)

"So the Lord blessed the latter end of Job more than his beginning, for he had fourteen thousand sheep and six thousand camels and a thousand yoke of oxen, and a thousand she asses." (v12)

Had Satan the accuser, known what the outcome would be, he would not have asked permission to attack Job.

> **Had Satan the accuser, known what the outcome would be, he would not have asked permission to attack Job.**

No wonder the apostle Paul announced in Romans 8:28, *"And we know that all things work together for good to them that love God, to them who are the called according to his purpose."*

Believers, we do not deny the fact that we go through hardship and difficulties. We cry and suffer loss. There are issues and struggles for which there are no answers. But due to the fact that we have a great high priest in the heavens who intercedes on our behalf and, due to the fact that our God works all things for our good, therefore He knows how to strengthen and keep us during the storms of life.

He turns our weeping into joy and makes us smile again. We must thank and praise His Holy Name for His everlasting kindness and mercy towards us.

I therefore conclude by saying that what the devil meant for evil, God turns it around for the good of the believer. Therefore be encouraged, knowing that your life and times are in the hands of the Judge of "The Supreme Court of Heaven"!

Bishop Glen Ferguson (Author)
Founder & Senior Pastor
Faith Dimensions Ministries

If you have ever found yourself in an impossible situation, where no amount of prayer and fasting seem to move that mountain, this book is for you.

Bishop Glen's insightful and anointed preaching on this subject has been life-changing for many followers of Christ and is now available in book form; a manual for breakthrough where circumstances appear insurmountable.

'The Supreme Court of Heaven', with its biblical examples, and practical application will open the way for you to boldly approach the throne room and experience God's favour.

Chris Kembrey

Made in the USA
Coppell, TX
11 December 2024

42260764R00056